BEFORE THE BURNING

BEFORE THE BURNING

Elaine Woodruff

Mellen Poetry Press
a division of
Mellen University Press
Lewiston/Queenston/Lampeter/Berlin/Salzburg/Grand Turk

Library of Congress Cataloging-in-Publication Data

Woodruff, Elaine.
  Before the burning / Elaine Woodruff.
     p. cm.
  ISBN 0-7734-2718-X
  I. Title.
  PS3573.O62638B4   1994
  811'.54--dc20   93-46258
                                                        CIP

Mellen Poetry Press
The Edwin Mellen Press
Box 450
Lewiston, New York 14092

Printed in the United States of America

For Robert and David

CONTENTS

BEFORE THE BURNING

I

Afraid? Of whom am I afraid?

Not death, for who is he?

Emily Dickinson

SWEET GENTLE POET OF SCARRED LANGUAGE

God is not here for him. Nor will be.
Except when running through woods in words
only, silently screaming for heartwood.

He wants to be in love, but cannot.
Knows commitment, once committed, is
loss. His lover, poetry, weans herself on his darkness.

Slender hands and a scalloped ear lobe
invite caresses, remind he has
never been tough enough for himself. He

sharpens words on razor straps and whittles
thoughts till they sting, but quietly,
then no one will notice until afterwards.

Consumed in sadness, he dies now,
slowly, rather than waiting for an end. This
keeps him from being afraid of death, temporarily.

When he really dies he will be wrapped in words
before the burning. Afterwards, she will
scatter whatever is left.

EXILES

Who hasn't seen the stars
hanging from the trees?
Octavio Armand

Suffering from a transient disease,
the oriental woman hears the voice of her
husband's mistress blow across her inner ear.
Without further warning she pulls her children
to drown in an ocean they soundlessly kick.

Falling into the waves' edge, the son dies
a crustacean thrown to the elements.
The girl remains to remind her father
and his lover of mother's truncation.
Living, in spite of her invitation

to the sea to swallow her, the mother
struggles with her exile, learns, late,
her desperate feelings have numbed her.
A snail carrying its home, she seeks
solace in a hospital. Thirsty for his family

her husband comes daily to catch her hand,
search her with sea eyes. Hoping
to see home, he sees waves washing it away.
The mistress, alone in her water world
fills ashtrays with broken white snails,

drinks drafts of sea water. Seaweed
outlines her teeth and hangs from her head.
Branded by the sea, she sinks into herself.
Exile can be arcadia: walls become windows.
Sometimes, but not necessarily.

"Life is paid back in your staggering debt of fear."
Pablo Neruda

CATHERINE STEVENS BORRON
1917-1983

I.

Our hands are locked
I, trying to supply your
last hour
you, pulling energy
from the blood in my palm and fingers.

The warmth of your cold hand
confuses
makes me yearn
for my first position
when I, in a curl
tapped your blood
through the cord
still unsevered.

Burning in our umbilical bind
I swallow throat tears.

Whose fear
is it
that ties our hands,
that keeps the cord
intact?

Are you afraid
of letting me go
or are you afraid of going
without me
or are you afraid
for me?

I do not want to know
what I want to know: What is
entering death like?
But I do want to know
what you do not want me to know:
what is entering death
like for you?

Your hands get colder.
As you press your fingers closer,
I look at your brown eyes
mocking fear.
My glance falls to the comfortable
brown spots on your hands.

Thoughts crowd out each other
fall
one by one
to the grip of my stomach
where the knot is eased
only by the nearness of your death
and knowing
now is too precious for my pain.

II.

Christmas
I come home
to look for you.
You are in the china cups
the music box
and the pink silk peonies
on the dining room table
but you are not moving in the hall
or cutting pastry in the kitchen.

You shopped early.
I sit holding my gift.

I play carols to an empty room,
talk when no one is around.

I think of your hand
the touch on my forehead
when I was sick
the hands that painted,
kept your design in every room.

I study the paintings.

The desk is still strewn
with your articles, news columns, editorials
your byline on Kennedy's death.

I look at your sewing machine.
Put back on my white Easter skirt
and gold blouse you fitted for me.
I remember the hand-tailored clothes
you mailed to me at college
feel the love between
the stitches of those years.

I stand in front of the crucifix
nailed to your bedroom wall.
The strips of palm you stuck behind it
are covered with dust.
I smell the burned palm.

I am sorry, for you, that
your children
no longer hang crucifixes,
burn prayers.

This is our reality,
another Christmas at home.

III.

To death
and back
you await my arrival.
Conscious, again, you mumble
my green sweater is pretty.
I owe you something.
Neither of us know.

Father takes your other hand.
Your eyes flicker
approval of being
stretched for your cross
by a husband and child
who hurry you in your death.

Your hand could paint
this last scene.
But the flowers from your oils
are never wilted
and the trees are lush
or at least waiting
for re-birth in spring.

Gasping brings
your other children.
Virginia bathes your head.
Rosemary wipes
the white from the corners
of your unlatched mouth.
James covers your feet.
Gerald, deliberately,
straightens the sheet.
Stephen takes your pulse
whispering to John the
low number they dread.

You leave us with your
body of love mingled
with smells of death.
No apotheosis.

I squeeze your limp hand
trying to pump
part of the blood you gave me
back into your body.
But the doctor says "no"
and I let go
of your hand.

Frightens me to think of the diamondback
Rattlers down in the earth with you.

BURIED IN DIAMOND EARRINGS

You left me with your other special
pair (buried in the Civil War
to be saved with the silver.)

An aunt wore them, then you,
now they grace my ears:
wreaths of engraved gold with dangling balls

suspended on delicate chains--just as they were
for more than a hundred years.
A year and a half later, Mother,

what are you like down there?
Would I know you still? Or find
diamonds sparkling in a nest of dust?

As I finger my new old gold
I hold you a moment.
Dread of diamondbacks disappears.

Now you slither from my thoughts.
Your diamonds flash still
but I am losing your face.
Dark eyes, taut bronze skin,
hair, silver streaked. . .

EARLY DARKNESS: WEST BERLIN, 1965

Sun rays chipped rust
from Herr Reiman's field glasses
and made them slippery
in his calloused palm.
Swiping them against his grey sleeve,
he raised them
again
to his watery eyes.

Since dawn
he had been waiting
on the splintered platform
for a glimpse of his wife and son
on the other side of The Wall,
silently staring to a silent
audience.

He would wait,
watch.

He had come in
trench coat
grey flannels,
and today
his lederhosen
matted the hair on his legs
as he lifted and lowered
the glasses.

He looked.

For diversion on these Saturdays
and Sundays,
he would turn his left side to The Wall
and stare
at the human lines half a kilometer away
at Checkpoint Charlie.

Mostly he spotted
laughing Americans
wearing colored hats
as they pushed their way inside the gates.
They sometimes returned frowning,
but they left.

Herr Reiman again faced
The Wall.

Frequently he rubbed
his hand across the top of The Wall and
wished that his life were not like the broken glass
embedded in the cement.

And when his arms ached
with weariness from holding
the glasses in position,
he would imagine Lotte and Franz
ripping their stomachs
as he helped them
cross the Wall:

standing on the platform
he had even traced Lotte's lips
and once caught himself
tossing his young son
in the air.

Then the glasses banged against his chest
reminding him
to steady them again to
look at the pocked buildings
topped with red flags.

Dusk yielded to darkness.

Never able to ignore
whispering couples,
weathered billboards
with the boyish Kennedy
promising
"Ich bin ein Berliner,"
Herr Reiman began his trek
across the western sector
to his home and older son, Karl.

Passing dinner clubs,
he heard waltzes in doorways,
shadows danced about him in counterpoint.
He stumbled over a kneeling sidewalk artist,
smeared red and purple chalk
on his bare leg:
Herr Reiman marred a modern Christ ministering
his Last Supper.

Then he was home.

FIGURES AT THE CONVENT OF ST. WALBURGA

> In the heart of the West is a small
> settlement with twenty German nuns.

Oil, still dripping from the saint's
sacred crypt in Germany, is flown
to Boulder, Colorado, sold
in small vials to believers and non
while Walburga's avowed brides of
Christ take their turn
at kitchen, tractor and milking
to keep their convent farm in bread and butter.
Tight-scheduled women flowing
in black, fold white hands six times daily.
Matins, while lovers still sleep.

Light through the stained glass
distorts the halo of one child-bride
at chapel. Though nineteen other forms
in black and white seem the same,
her darkened eyes betray serenity.
Mother Superior is distracted
by sour notes from her young voice,
discord of a chaste mind
dissatisfied with "I do."
Yet the oil still drips in Germany.
That is solvent enough for her marriage.

19

II

Music, when soft voices die,

Vibrates in the memory.

Shelley

FOR FRANZ XAVER SÜSSMAYER

REQUIEM

Christ's blood gives life through death
in the sacrifice of the mass. Divinity, his
humanness: his flesh becomes our death as we drop
randomly like oranges from a juggler's learning hands.
Others take our place to keep the word alive. Süssmayer
finishes Mozart's REQUIEM. I have too long
lamented the deaths of five soulmates.
They live in death. I died in life.
We look to the resurrection.
David Lively plays a private concert in the
penthouse of Phyllis and Aron Katz. Paintings
hang acoustically framing sounds from the
grand piano giving color to Mendelssohn, Debussy.
David will be in Paris tomorrow but tonight
he offers music before a Roman feast.

I.

KYRIE

Charlie, strutting into mass
wears striped bib overalls, dress shoes, red-white-
blue tennis band on his shaved head. Wrinkled as a
Chinese dog, he prays for the sick and homeless.

II.

DIES IRAE

We are caught
in the jealousy
of life where in-
sults fly about
the room, silent
notes from a baby grand.

The melody seems
simple; not so
the day of wrath.
Is God
angry with us
for trying to
replace him?

I say "mea culpa,"
you say "mea culpa,"
not soon enough.
Reconciliation
never waits.

III.

TUBA MIRUM

We shall tremble before
the trumpet's mighty blast.
OLD TESTAMENT

Thirteen third graders from Rosemary
Lohndorf's class ride the bus to Denver
without getting black marks against
their names. I chaperone. They learn
about history, the record of death. Mariah, Danielle,
and Star are fascinated by the stasis in the dioramas.
They forget about death. The miners'
wives are scrubbing clothes on cold rocks
in the stream, babies in floursack dresses
bear designs of coal dust from playing
in a coal cart. Beyond the diorama a portrait of
spectacled Augusta Tabor hangs beside ones
of Senator Tabor and Baby Doe. The saddest
story. Fifty, fighting, and tired, Mrs.
Tabor weeps in court at the sound of her
divorce decree. She would like
to take Nobel's newly-invented dynamite
to blow up the melodrama in her life, begin again.
She claims her husband. But Baby Doe, a beauty
from Black Hawk, jumps her claim, becomes
the new bride of Senator Tabor.

David, André, Scott, and August are intrigued
by mining equipment. They touch jackhammers,
Davy Lamps, and pans of fool's gold.
They hold chunks of midnight coal.
They see the difference in silver and gold.
Silver made Silver King Tabor
a fortune, and gold lost it for him. Widowed
Baby Doe was left to freeze to death
outside his mine. (Women were feared inside.)

The other six students, playing with coal as they listen,
hear a lecture about the bad effects
of coal dust, the early deaths of children
in company towns, and how silver is
parasitical, clings to other
things, even turns black grabbing
oxygen in the air. A temporary
state waiting for polish. The children return
to school oblivious to their streaked hands.

IV.

REX TREMENDAE

Between reality and the imagination
I stir the supernatural into the natural
the natural into the supernatural.
The brew is bitter and I am afraid.
Memory believes nothing is more terrible.
So I ease my mind with distractions,
white horses pushing snow into form:
a pure, eternal bed to lie upon.
But I am cold, the bed is big. I am alone,
I see rows of beds beside me though no one
is resting upon them. I pray to the Lady
of Silence, receive no answer. Before the
poem ends I want to roll off the bed into
assurance wrapped in warm blankets.
The sun comes out to tease. Forgetting
possibilities I scoop snow over my bare
body and find the coldness warm enough
to suffice. Dark pieces of dullness fly
about my head chanting "there is nothing
false. Love is always." What is the country
of this distance that keeps me home from
myself? Rain dissolves magic dust in the air
of my consciousness. I breathe sunshine
into hope between the showers. The
thunder rumbles its timelessness into winter
afternoons turned spring. When is the night
over? King of Fearful majesty, save me.

V.

RECORDARE

Pink blossoms on the pima cotton
a puppy's tongue licking bare thighs
exposed soles on mounds of warm earth
seeping mouthfuls of spring rain
these sensations of childhood
bring memories of kneeling
praying fervently without knowing
why pretending to address great
weeping crowds who smiled only
when I waved my white handkerchief
and delivered consoling words
I was my own savior and theirs

VI.

CONFUTATIS

I witness a story of once-sensitive lovers
living in wrong. Damned, their wedlock became
a contest of wills, willfully spiteful. She called
her husband Holy Polyphemus. Keeping his
eye open, her cyclops kept watch as if
observation might see her to death. The
sacrament of marriage would only allow him to wait
for, not hasten, her end. At night the wife
slept in wakefulness, closed-eyed,
anger searing in sore pores, hate
plinking strains on nerve strings.

If his hands could touch the braille face
she pictures, he would feel a love current.
But he has no hands for softness, and she
has no eyes for defense. Two cripples,
they stumble thirstily on a bed of prickly talk,
forgetting pentimento, the oasis.

Waking her in blackness he converts
a dream, lets her play lead:
transubstantiation for his feed.
Light lifts the two in godless communion.
A burnt prayer rises with dawn.

VII.

LACRYMOSA

Draped in blue and purple for Palm Sunday passion,
I played a poor peasant woman, but one rich
for having seen the disciples of Jesus with their Master.
Peter's denial, three times. Could have been thirteen.

My words over, I sat round-shouldered upon a stool,
awaited Jesus stumbling with his cross down the sloping
aisle. Beads rose on his brow. I trembled as the pipe
organ breathed, choir queried "Were You There?"

I met Jesus at the steps of the sanctuary,
lifted his face with gentle hands, and wept.
Others wept, you would have wept
as I bathed his face.

VIII.

DOMINE JESU

Red plastic flowers
decorate the tombstones.
Only dates are different.
Nobody in that town
died on the same day
or gave first cries together.

Stringy evergreens
line the yard
(probably planted too close)
and no flower lives.
Caliche holds the fence
enclosing pale dust plots.

My shoes crunch the struggling
grass across grey graves.
I see if anyone is watching,
kneel to say a prayer.
Lord Jesus, where are you,
Lord Jesus?

IX.

HOSTIAS

A victim in a dream
I am on the sea
with seaweed ribbons swishing
out of the green to caress me.
Soon softness of ribbons
turns to stinging strings
slapping my face.
No one hears my words.

Raw wind lifts smothered sound.
I stand naked.
A seabird pecks holes
in my hands and feet.
The breeze clogs my breath
with brine. I weave
my wreath from whipping skeins.
O Lord accept my sacrifice.

X.

SANTUS

Man is a spirit who tries for answers.
He knows most when the rehearsal concludes
but he knows the curtain never drops,
except temporarily.

Where does earth end
and Heaven begin?
Angels sing on freeways,
sinners play eternal harps.
A galloping cat frightens
the lady on the train.
Unaware of love's freeing
power a fairy sets the
death sentence as fair
for a humane capitalist.
What fool prefers
school to the heavenly city?
My advice to young children is this: believe only
what you cannot know,
cannot see. Logic
is less than bereavement.

Being without hope gives
reason for hope. All
things pass, as did
Mozart, and his task
was passed on to his inferior who made his REQUIEM
superior. Even the bereaved
swan prefers counting fish in the lucid lake
to taking Spanish school.
Some sad souls
study hard to deserve
death. "Dear Amadeus,
where are you?"
I want a life that tells me
where a black hearse
delivers death.
"Coeur Simple," the wind
whispers, "you are looking
for miracles." I stretch my neck
toward the Son. Christ
is metamorphosis,
glory closing gaps.
Holy, holy, holy.

XI.

BENEDICTUS

This, first was to be a river
poem. Variations arose. Air
is sweetest that contains a peacock,
a transfigured bird who needs no grape cure.

The country of a thousand years of peace
had no octopus, no olive grove
only lovers and some negatives
housed at the nearby CAMERA.

Looking for renewal the priest
makes a narrow escape, sees
Salome in the mirror,
leaves on the 12:10 for Amsterdam.

A laboratory poem may be
what this turns out to become.
Whatever, three chores will be
fulfilled, the cruise, the doodler,
of course, other-world voices.

Swimming by night is even better. Smile once
for Yeats, once for Proust. "Drop your gown, Maisie.
Between us there is nothing, if not violent
pastoral, a broken home with a carpet not bought."

Even the ugliest, fattest people
go out to lunch. How can a poem survive
amid such dissonance? They are poetry as are tulips.
Blessed. I must sing this like a fever.

XII.

AGNUS DEI

I peek over the edge of my small love
into the love of others. Strange
animals, they break up time-worn
lairs, divide children--sticks
of furniture from attics of rusted memories.
Only reflections of strawberries, sandals
cool the throat and feet of the observed.

Frustrated, I see that new direction
is more than I can find in exteriors.
Transfiguration becomes human metamorphosis.
Is reality a miracle? Or a miracle reality?
Only imagination knows--
yet, never knows it knows.
Wolfgang is sometimes Franz.

III

This life is but the passage of a day,

This life is but a pang and all is over...

Christina Rossetti

CHAMELEON FINGERTIPS

I read the lines in my hand
to find who I am
in this world of poetry.
Am I a lady with a falcon
or a lady with a unicorn?
A baroque image of the nativity
reflects an eidetic Dutch interior
of a Japanese print--then
is this a nursery rhyme?
I float through an Italian garden
behind an eerie mirror. A specter,
you are no child with a cello.
I take an evening walk in France
search for composition but
these haunting images remain.
Tia Maria, Tia Maria, Tia Maria,
I sip the sound from a paper doily,
an exchange of transparent gifts.

Death and lovers sat smoking
at the table hearing evening music
like a light left on in an autumn sonnet.
A moth storms the angels of night
divorcing swans and bats
tossing time like air
in the face of strangers.
Solitude eludes. My life line's
the same, but my fingertips change.
The dream begins with an Easter
letter to a nun who died
on All Souls Day. Her burial
made death void of grief for her
but turned me to chase
winter's carol in a search
for permanence. Given home
I make nightly journeys past
the myths of Joan and realize
how cruel Humpty Dumpty
was treated by all the men.
A broken bird, caged for antiquity,
he could have sung on a summer night.

The Garden of Childhood
is my child's Japan
the first autumn of the first snow
building a house of winter.

Easter will bring fairy dust of
grapes turned raisins, guests in
metaphysical gardens bearing seasons.
Waterfalls of the living
convert to stone walls
who wake from torture
when the night watch
sings Indian ballads. These
somber songs bind dragons
send Phoenixes flying
and the Furies amiss. Ma Mère!
Why this nostalgia for India
like some giant in a garden
of naked frogs on angels' wings?

Praying working
an intruding self becomes
a lyric looking for itself
in this nightmare of possibilities,
a plastic index to temporality.
I yearn for the lie,
truth and beauty to dissolve
in randomness made permanent,
but my hand is only
which part of the story?

PIETÀ

"...this baby terrified you? I
despise the fear which is pure
terror in a mind unreasoning."
        Hecuba, THE TROJAN WOMEN

Child of woe, a mother
picks up your broken body,
laments your useless bruises
when she sends
her own son to war.
"What fear mounts

high enough for this?"
she moans as she bends in a kiss.
Her own grandson is only
one, but also every child.
No reason for war
could persuade her

her armfuls of death
cradle justice.
Thrown from a tower to appease
a king, you Astyanax,
have survived through centuries of guilt.

Menelaus' sin is unforgivable.
Not only the Trojan
women know this.

Draping her arms with your death,
Hecuba wildly wept.
Locked in centuries of your memory,
a mother grieves still.

LETTER FROM HONG KONG

*"One of the basic decisions of coming on
mission was to attempt to put all at risk, to let
go of the safe, the familiar."*
                    Ann McCusker, Lay Missionary

Far from neighborhood picnics
in your bermuda shorts and Irish
smile, you find a new home
in a city of noise where you
are searching for deep peace.
At forty you begin learning
Cantonese from instructors at
Asia/Yale-in-China Language Center.
Years of English, Latin, French,
do not help your seven tones.
You know you are too old to become fluent.
Depressed, you take a ride on Star Ferry

contemplate your new scene:
fascinated by bays and beaches, you
want to swim but not in polluted
water. Elegant mansions with views
of the South China Sea cling to the hillsides
near shacks where families share one room
above a garden. More Rolls and Mercedes
than in any other city
jam the streets, hold up buses
filled with poor farmers
carrying live ducks. Skyscrapers cast shadows
on poverty. But there are children everywhere and

citizens who light joss sticks and ask favors
from gods. You take the ferry back
to the din and long lines that disappear
at sundown. "At night the lights of the city
and hundred of ships in the harbor make it
beautiful." Like typhoon
warning flags, your spiritual
barometer goes up and down, tests
you daily in your desire to come home
to the Rockies. But you end
your letter on a cheerful note, "As
the Irish say, 'God bless.' "

That is what you say.
Anxiety punctuates your letter, reveals
(what I already know)
in the wavering handwriting: an adopted child
looking for a home. The severing
of the sacrament of two marriages cuts
through your words to unsteady hands.
A life noisy, like Hong Kong, searches
for serenity in the clutter of glitz and pain.

Looking for God in this exotic city
you clamor through experiences to please Him
forgetting the gentle you is quite enough.

BRIDGE ACROSS MARAIS DE CYGNE

in Butler County, Missouri, is the first
suspension bridge in the state.
Grandfather Edward Barnes Borron
designed and built it in 1903
just before he took his bride,
twenty years younger, in a covered
wagon to a dry Texas farm.

I suspect those are the only
facts Grandmother told us.
From a colored picture taken
eighty-four years later,
I see the river is red, muddy,
and is but a marsh. The bridge is not
the massive structure I was told.

I did a lot of guessing
about my grandfather.
Grandmother filled in the blanks.
I know his moustache smelled of coffee
When I sat on his knee, and children
were not to touch his violin or books.
I knew, foremost, he built the bridge.

Grandmother met "Daddy"
in the boarding house where she worked.
Sixteen and friendly she
served the gentleman's breakfast.
Later, stole into his empty room
where she tried to read his book titles
and fell in love with his books.

She sang the shy professor into marriage
with her sweet Irish songs. A wedding picture
tells lies about their two decades difference
and her eighth grade graduation.
Her hair in a pompadour, she appears elegant
in a white dress with a rose.

WALKING INTO THE NOW

*God did not give us a spirit of timidity
but a spirit of power and love and discipline.*
                              2 Timothy 1:7

Rounding off the corners of good
taste, I decline the offering, shrink
into the air and broom the spiders
hanging on angled cobwebs, a close-in

of the beginning. We live between
houses no matter whose fireplace
burns. The smoke of then is black
up the chimney, yet waits

to be burned off.
An angel wings out of the coals
and announces dinner in a broken
room of uninvited guests.

Dead color is all that remains
of the fire. Outside, boulders edging
night pose threats of falling upward
into the sky without notice.

Mythical songs in an eternal city
are fishnets for our scared thoughts.
Geese flying over make us
comfortable though south is no adequate

answer for where they go.
Will they be interviewed
in Mexico? And when do they north again?
Do they ask the ornithologists?

Lying in our lairs of deceit,
we can lure the sky to cover us
with its fallen stars, but we must survive
now cuddled to a stellarless night.

ABOUT THE AUTHOR

Born and raised in Texas, Elaine Woodruff studied English at Our Lady of the Lake University in San Antonio. She was in creative writing programs at the University of Alaska in Fairbanks, where she received an M.F.A. degree, and the University of Denver, where she received a Ph.D. in English. Elaine now lives in Boulder, Colorado.